# Getting @ of Wrinkles

by Teena Raffa-Mulligan
illustrated by Craig Smith

## Blake
### EDUCATION
*Better ways to learn*

# Characters

Great Gran

Great Grandpop

Tessa

Amelia

2

# Contents

# Chapter 1

# Nibble Dust!

Tessa's Great Grandma Em had a face like a sheet of scrunched-up newspaper. She had so many wrinkles that Tessa couldn't count them and had given up trying. Great Grandpop Alfred teased Great Grandma Em lots.

"You look like a hippopotamus that has been bathing in the river too long," he said at breakfast.

"The bags under your eyes could carry the treasure from a sunken pirate ship," Great Grandpop Alfred said at lunch.

"The furrows on your face are deep enough for next season's wheat crop," he said at dinner.

Great Grandma Em didn't get upset. She peered over her glasses at him. "Your bald head is so shiny it could show ships the way to shore on a moonless night," she said. "I'd rather have a face like crumpled newspaper."

Tessa loved spending school holidays on the farm with her great-grandparents. They were fun and made her laugh. Mum and Dad said they were 'real characters'.

"They're a bit unusual," Mum said as she packed Tessa's backpack for another visit.

Dad grinned. "You can say that again."

"You're a very lucky girl," Tessa's mum said. "Not everyone your age has great-grandparents to visit."

The trip from the city to the country seemed to take forever. Even with puzzle books and colouring in to do, Tessa got so bored she fell asleep and had to be woken up when they finally arrived.

"Maybe she needs a kiss from a Prince Charming," she heard Great Grandpop Alfred say.

"You'd better go and get one of the frogs from the creek, then," Great Grandma Em told him.

Tessa giggled. It was great to be back. Now she had two whole weeks of fun to look forward to. They had planned so many exciting things to do during their phone calls about her stay.

First on the list, after they watched her parents' van disappear in the distance, was to help Great Grandma Em bake a super-special chocolate cake for dessert.

They went straight to the kitchen, where Tessa had to hide under the table while everything went into the huge mixing bowl.

"Don't peek," Great Grandma Em said. "It's a secret recipe and not even you can see what goes into the mixture."

"You wouldn't want to know anyway," Great Grandpop chuckled. "She learned it from a witch and it's full of magic things that Em thinks will make her skin as smooth as a baby's bottom."

Great Gran snorted. "Nibble dust!" She put the last of the mixture in the cake tin, popped it into the oven to bake and then handed Tessa the bowl and spoon to lick. "I don't give two hoots about wrinkles."

# Chapter 2

# Wrinkle Remedies

That was before the letter arrived from her best friend, Amelia.

When they got the mail early the next morning, Tessa couldn't stop staring at the letter. It was on really thin paper folded to make its own envelope. Great Gran said it was called an aerogram and had come all the way from America.

When she read it, Great Gran got so excited she danced Tessa all the way around the yard singing "Hoorah! Hoorah!" in her loudest voice. The racket made the dogs howl and sent the chooks into a terrible flap.

Then, Great Gran stopped so suddenly Tessa almost did a somersault over the feed bin.

"Gadzooks and gadzillion," groaned Great Gran. "I haven't seen Amelia for fifty years. Not since we were young women. She was such a beauty. All the young men adored her. They would line up from her dad's farm to the rabbit-proof fence for one of her smiles."

Tessa could see a story coming. She perched on the fence, her eyes shining eagerly. "And?"

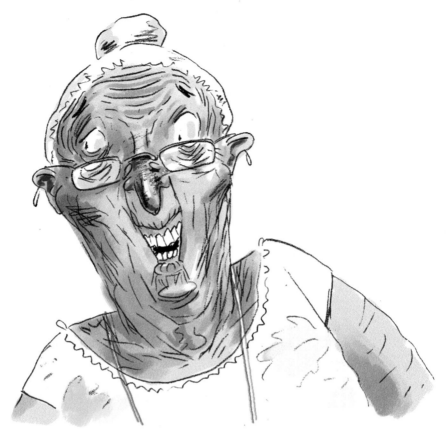

It was all Great Gran needed to get her started. She had a faraway look on her face. "Amelia could have chosen any one of the boys we knew but she fell in love with an American sailor we met at the Christmas Eve dance. They were married just four weeks later because he had to go back to sea. Amelia looked lovely in a sky-blue suit. I wore a pink dress and caught her bouquet of flowers."

"A few days later, I went to the harbour to say goodbye to them and waved my handkerchief until the ship was a tiny speck on the ocean."

"And you haven't seen her since?" Tessa asked.

Great Gran sighed. "Not once. We've always written to each other and sent birthday and Christmas cards. Photos too, in the early days when our children were small."

"When your dad had the phone put on for us, I called her a few times. It was wonderful to hear her voice. And now she's coming to visit. I should be pleased."

Great Gran checked the letter again. "Of course I am pleased. But what will I do? I can't let her see me like this. I've got just ten days to get rid of my wrinkles."

Tessa bounced down off the fence. "Don't worry, I'll help."

They hurried indoors. Great Gran let Tessa draw a big circle on the calendar around the date when Amelia was due to arrive.

They ate the rest of the super-special chocolate cake and a whole tub of ice-cream to help them think.

"I've got an idea," said Tessa. "If you stand on your head, you might unwrinkle, like when Mum hangs creased clothes on a hanger."

Great Gran nodded. "That might work. But it's been such a long time since I did anything like that, you'd better catch my legs."

Tessa missed.

"Timber!" cried Great Grandpop when Great Gran toppled sideways.

Now she had a headache as well as wrinkles, and had to lie on the sofa for a while before they tried something else.

That gave Tessa time to think. "Steam," she said at last. "That gets the crinkles out really well when Mum's doing the ironing."

It didn't work on Great Gran's face. She leaned over a bowl of steaming water with a towel covering her head for an hour. Afterwards, she felt so hot that she almost fainted and had to lie down again.

She felt worse when Great Grandpop marched about the house singing, 'Emma, the Red-faced Grandma' to the tune of 'Rudolph the Red-nosed Reindeer'.

# Chapter 3

# The Best Idea Yet

"Never mind, Great Gran," said Tessa. "I don't care that you've got wrinkles."

Great Gran wailed, "But I do! Have you any other idea how I can get rid of them?"

Tessa thought for a minute. "You could try fruit and vegetable juice. Mum says it's really good for hair, eyes and skin. If you have it for breakfast, lunch and dinner, surely that would make a difference."

It was great fun picking the fruit from the trees and gathering the vegetables from the garden. Tessa and Great Grandpop had competitions to see who was the fastest fruit and vegetable picker. The winner got to press the button on the juicing machine. It was Tessa every time. She also shared a little of the juice.

Great Gran drank almost enough to fill the farm dam, and after a couple of days her face was as green as the drink she was drinking.

"You look like a seasick hippopotamus that has been bathing in the river too long and then taken a boat trip," said Great Grandpop.

Great Gran moaned, "Ooh, I feel like it, too. There has to be another way."

"What about this Nine-minute Miracle Mud Mask?" Tessa pointed to a bottle in the bathroom. "If it can work wonders in less than ten minutes, think what it would do if you left it on all night."

The next morning Tessa was woken by a loud yell from her great-grandparents' bedroom.

"It's all right," Great Grandpop said when she skidded up to their doorway. "I thought I was in bed with a monster. It's just your Great Gran."

Next, Great Gran tried using a whole tub of vanilla and blueberry yoghurt on her face, but that scared the neighbours.

Little Robbie Beetson ran up the hill as if he was in an Olympic race, and Mrs Mills, who had gone for a walk without her glasses, thought the aliens had landed. It took three cups of sweet tea and four freshly baked scones to calm her down.

After she left, Great Gran and Tessa sat on the verandah, thinking. They watched the gate swinging back and forth and the trees blowing about.

"There's a storm brewing," said Great Gran. "The wind's picking up."

Tessa jumped to her feet. "That's it! The wind! It will blow your wrinkles out."

"How?" Great Gran looked puzzled.

"Like on a clothes line. Sheets that have been hanging out to dry on a windy day don't have any wrinkles. If it works with them, it can work with your face." Tessa's eyes gleamed. It was the best idea yet.

Great Gran didn't think so. "You're not hanging me on any clothes line. Especially in a storm."

"We don't need to. All you have to do is put your head out the window when the wind is strongest and let it blow right in your face."

It took Tessa the rest of the afternoon to
convince Great Gran that she should give it a try.
By that time, the wind was icicle chilly and
howling about the farmhouse.

Within minutes of letting it blow on her face,
Great Gran's skin had turned blue and her teeth
were chattering louder than a tree full of
parrots. The wrinkles were just as deep as ever.

# Chapter 4

# Madame Amazia's Special Potion

Later, when they were all sitting before a blazing fire drinking mugs of hot chocolate and listening to the rain drum on the roof, Tessa shook her head. "I've run out of ideas."

"Me too," Great Gran sighed. "I'm never going to get rid of my wrinkles." She was still feeling miserable the next day, even though the storm had passed and the sun was shining.

Great Grandpop fetched the keys to the truck.
"I know what will cheer you up, Em. There's a fair
in town. While you're having fun you'll forget all
about your wrinkles."

The first person Tessa saw at the fair was a
gypsy woman sitting on a chair outside a caravan.
The sign said, 'Madame Amazia — ask and you
shall be told'.

She grabbed Great Gran's arm. "I bet she can
help you get rid of your wrinkles. Gypsies are like
fairies, they know magic."

"I suppose it's worth a try," said Great Gran.

Madame Amazia took them inside her caravan and listened carefully. She shone a bright light onto Great Gran's face and studied every wrinkle. With a smile, she nodded. "I have just the thing. My special potion will turn back the clock in ten days."

Great Gran only had five until Amelia arrived but she said, "I'll take it."

It looked dreadful and smelled worse. Great Gran took a deep breath and swallowed her first dose as soon as they left the gypsy's caravan. Then she and Tessa went to find Great Grandpop and enjoy the fun of the fair.

Once they had had enough of toffee apples, fairy floss, lemonade, rides and games, they piled into the truck to go home. By the time they reached the main road, Great Gran's white hair had turned grey. It was black by suppertime.

# Chapter 5

# Meeting Amelia

"Wow!" breathed Tessa. "It's working."

Great Gran took a double dose.

By lunchtime the next day, she didn't need her glasses to read Aunt Edith's new recipe for pumpkin and apple pudding.

By dinnertime, she could hear the Dibben twins whispering outside the chicken coop in the backyard when they tried to take Hennie's eggs. And her hearing aid was still in the bathroom!

Next, Great Gran noticed her knees had stopped creaking and her back was unbent. She threw away her walking stick and danced an Irish jig with Tessa.

Great Grandpop joined in. "That's amazing," he said. "But you still have your wrinkles."

Great Gran looked in the mirror. He was right. She was running out of time. "Maybe I need a triple dose."

That did the trick.

By the time the big day arrived, Great Gran's skin was as smooth as whipped cream, her cheeks were as rosy as ripe strawberries and her eyes were like rich, dark, chocolate drops.

"You're as lovely as the day I first saw you running across the paddock from the Maloney's prize bull." Great Grandpop waltzed her around the living room.

"Nibble dust!" laughed Great Gran. "And put me down — Tessa and I have to find me something special to wear."

Amelia's train wasn't due to arrive until two. That left plenty of time for Tessa to help Great Gran take down the red, velvet curtains from the dining room window and sew a dress trimmed with the fringe from the table lamp and the buttons from the sofa cushions.

"Now we can go," said Great Gran.

Of course they were late.

The only person left waiting at the station when they arrived was a shrivelled, little, old lady with a face like a wrinkled prune.

Tessa stared. "That's not her, is it?"

Great Gran couldn't believe it either. "Is that really you, Amelia?" she asked.

Her friend sighed. "I'm afraid so. But you haven't changed a bit, Em. You don't look a day older than when I left town all those years ago. What's your secret?"

Great Gran chuckled. Great Grandpop chortled. Tessa giggled.

"It's a long story," said Great Gran as they helped Amelia to the truck. "I'll tell you all about it on the way to see my friend the gypsy."

# Glossary

### brewing
forming

### chortled
laughed softly

### coop
a house for animals such as chickens

### don't give two hoots
to not care at all

### fetched
went and brought something back

## furrows
deep wrinkles

## gypsy
somebody who moves
from place to place

## perched
sat on something
high up

## racket
loud noise

## shrivelled
small and wrinkled

## Teena Raffa-Mulligan

My favourite great-grandma joke:

Why did Great Grandma wear her hearing aid to bed?

Because Great Grandpop talked in his sleep and she didn't want to miss anything.

Actually, it's the only great-grandma joke I know, but here's one about chickens.

Why did the chicken stay out of the sun?

It didn't want to get fried.

## Craig Smith